WHO WAS BENJAMIN FRANKLIN?

US HISTORY AND GOVERNMENT

Children's American History

Speedy Publishing LLC
40 E. Main St. #1156
Newark, DE 19711
www.speedypublishing.com

In this book, we're going to talk about the amazing life of Benjamin Franklin. So, let's get right to it!

BENJAMIN FRANKLIN

WHO WAS BENJAMIN FRANKLIN?

Benjamin Franklin was one of the Founding Fathers of the United States. He was also an inventor and a scientist. He ran his own printing press and was a publisher. He was also a statesman, a politician, a diplomat, and a freemason, which means he was a member of a secret society based on brotherhood. He was known as a genius in his own time and is frequently described as the "First American."

BENJAMIN FRANKLIN'S EARLY LIFE

Benjamin Franklin's father, Josiah, had 17 children in total, 10 boys and 7 girls. He had 7 children during his first marriage to Anne Child. After he married Abiah Folger, he had 10 more children. Ben was the youngest son in the group and he was born on the 17th of January in 1706 and christened as Benjamin Josiah Franklin.

FRANKLIN IN LONDON, 1767

BOSTON LATIN SCHOOL

He was his father's 15th child. The Franklin family was living in the city of Boston in the America colony called the Massachusetts Bay Colony at the time that Franklin was born.

Benjamin's father had dreams that his son would become a minister and he sent the boy to the Boston Latin School. Ben was an excellent student and loved to learn and to read. He soaked up as much knowledge as possible. However, Josiah's business wasn't doing well, so he couldn't afford to continue to send Ben to school, so at age 10, Benjamin had to quit school.

He went to work helping his father in his shop, which sold candles and soap. In those days, making candles was a tedious process of dipping wicks into hot cauldrons of wax over and over. His father could see that Ben was bored. He didn't want his young son to become a seaman as some of his other sons had done, so when Ben was 12 years old, Josiah sent him to become an apprentice in a print shop that was owned by Ben's older brother James.

YOUNG BEN

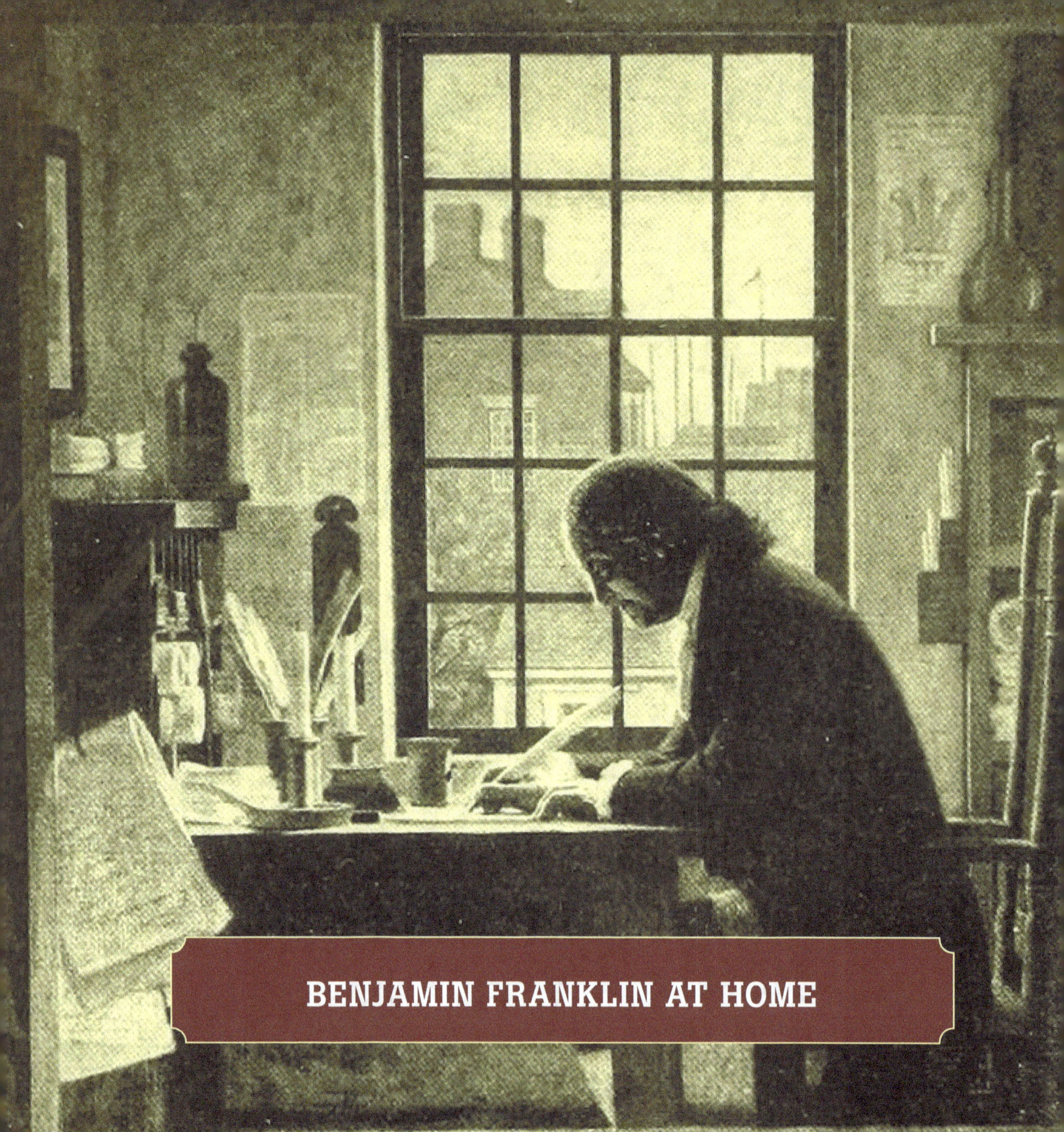

BENJAMIN FRANKLIN AT HOME

Printing and publishing went hand in hand in those days, and James was the publisher and printer of a newspaper called the "The New England Courant." Ben learned as much as he could about publishing. The newspaper often printed political pieces that were against the established, traditional politics and government. Ben picked up a lot of his political views during those years.

BENJAMIN FRANKLIN, 1746

Unfortunately, Ben's brother often mistreated him. He would beat Ben if he wasn't happy with something that Ben was doing.

At the age of 16, Ben was doing a lot of writing of his own and wanted to get it published in the newspaper. His brother refused, so Ben came up with a pen name.

He called himself "Mrs. Silence Dogood" and submitted more than a dozen letters to the press. His brother had no idea that it was Ben, so he published the letters, which were filled with Ben's imagination and clever witty sayings. Even though readers loved the letters, when James found out, he was absolutely furious.

BEN WORKING ON A PRINTING PRESS

BENJAMIN IN PHILADELPHIA

Finally, Ben had had enough of being abused. Even though he had a contract to continue his apprenticeship, Ben fled to New York at the age of 17 and eventually settled in Philadelphia, which would become his home on and off for the rest of his life.

LIFE IN LONDON

Ben was encouraged to start his own print shop and the governor of Pennsylvania offered to write him a letter of introduction so he could set up shop in London. So, Ben left for England and once there began the process of buying the materials he would need.

OLD LONDON
COACH
HATCHET

BENJAMIN FRANKLIN'S RESIDENCE IN LONDON, 1760

However, the promised letter never arrived and Benjamin had to take work at other print shops in London. While there, he soaked up the culture in England, by attending the theater, enjoying conversation over coffee with the local citizens, and reading as much as possible. He also crafted his own swimming flippers made of wood so he could do marathon swimming in the Thames River.

In 1725, he published his very first dissertation on Liberty. The essay argued that human beings didn't have free will.

Later in life, he disagreed with his earlier opinions and burned all the remaining pamphlets he could find. He kept just one copy for his records.

BACK TO PHILADELPHIA

Benjamin Franklin traveled back to Philadelphia from London in the year 1726. For several years he held different jobs. For a while he was a bookkeeper, then a shopkeeper. He went back to the trade of printing in 1728 and he was printing money for the government in New Jersey.

HOUSE IN WHICH BENJAMIN FRANKLIN LIVED

Later that year he went into business with a friend and they opened a print shop back in Philadelphia. They published books and

pamphlets for the government. In 1730, their printing establishment became Pennsylvania's official printer.

With the cash from his business and publications, Franklin was able to buy The Pennsylvania Gazette, which at the time was a failing newspaper. He changed it into the most popular newspaper in the thirteen colonies. It was one of the first newspapers to become profitable.

NKLIN
ELPHIA

BENJAMIN FRANKLIN COPPESS HOUSE

As he continued to make money, he bought real estate and other businesses. He did work for the community as well by organizing the first volunteer group to put out fires, which were a major hazard in the city.

POOR RICHARD'S ALMANACK

Toward the end of 1732, Franklin created a new publication. He authored it under the pen name Richard Saunders and called it "Poor Richard's Almanack."

POOR RICHARD'S ALMANAC ILLUSTRATED

RATTLE-SNAKE HERB.

THE *Indians* long made a Secret of the Herb they used in curing the Bite of that venemous Reptile a *RATTLE-SNAKE*: but since some curious Persons among the *English* have fully discover'd and are now well acquainted with it, I hope it will be an acceptable Service to these Parts of the World, if I make it more publick by the following Description, with the Figure of a Leaf of it.

THE Top and Branches of the Plant are thick set with small yellow Flowers in *August* & *September*. It is a Species of *Golden-Rod*, known from the other Sorts by the smoothness of the Leaf, and its pungent Taste, and occasioning when chewed & swallow'd, a small Stoppage of the Breath, and Contraction in the Throat; and the Stalk, which is in some Places less than a yard in height when at full Growth, in others more, is of a dull purple colour, and smooth, and cover'd with a fine blue Dust, like that on many of the English Plums. It grows in most Wood-Lands, but under the Shade of Trees is seldom rank or large, or with more than one, two or three Stalks. It is also found on the Banks of dry Ditches, & sometimes in them, & in Hedge-Rows: But it is most luxuriant near to Run Sides, if the Soil be rich, and not too moist, nor too much shaded. The Root continues over the Winter, and if set in a good Garden, will send forth (in the 2d or 3d Year) at least 50 Stalks. The Plant shoots early in the Spring & withers late in the Fall.

The *Indians* use it variously; sometimes they bruise [illegible]nes, sometimes chew it and spit in the Patient's Mouth, some lay it to the Wound, others about the Wound, sometimes they boil it and give the Water to drink, washing the Wound with it likewise: but always some of it is to be swallowed, either with the Spittle or with Water.

The Leaf figur'd in the Margin is one of the largest; for the most part they are not near so big though the Shape be the same.

Planets Motions for the 1, 8, 15, and 22 Days in each Month, 1737.

Mon.	Days	Sun's Place.	♄ ♊	♃ ♒	♂ ♉	♀ ♒	☿ ♑	Mon.	Sun's Place	♄ ♊	♃ ♓	♂ ♌	♀ ♊	☿ ♋
January	1	22 41	6	21	1	27	23	July	20♋8	20	23	18	14	D.
	8	29 49	5	23	5	♓	♒		26 48	21	23	2[illegible]	17	8
	15	6♒56	5	24	8	14	17		3♌28	22	23	27	21	14
	22	14 3	5	26	15	23	29		10 10	23	22	♍	26	24
February	1	24 11	5	29	17	♈	♓	August	19 15	23	22	7	♋	♌
	8	1♓15	5	♓	21	13	R.		26 30	24	21	12	10	27
	15	8 17	6	2	25	21	7		3♍14	25	20	16	17	♍
	22	15 18	6	3	25	29	1		10 0	25	19	21	24	23
March	1	22 17	6	5	♊	♐	D	September	19 44	26	18	27	♌	♎
	8	29 14	7	7	8	14	♓		26 34	26	17	♎	13	19
	15	6♈9	7	8	12	22	8		3♎26	26	16	6	20	28
	22	13 3	8	10	16	29	17		10 20	26	15	11	28	♏
April	1	22 51	9	12	22	♊	♈	October	19 15	26	14	17	♍	R.
	8	29 41	10	13	26	14	3		26 13	26	14	22	17	11
	15	6♉29	10	15	♋	19	14		3♏13	26	14	26	26	3
	22	13 15	11	16	5	24	♉		10 14	26	15	♏	♎	♎
May	1	21 55	12	18	10	28	♊	Novemb.	20 18	25	13	8	16	♏
	8	28 39	13	19	14	♋	14		27 23	25	14	12	25	10
	15	5♊21	14	20	19	♊	26		4♐29	24	14	17	♏	21
	22	12 3	15	21	23	27	♋		11 36	24	14	22	[illegible]	♐
June	1	21 35	16	22	29	21	14	December	20 47	23	15	28	[illegible]	15
	8	28 15	17	22	♌	17	R.		27 55	22	16	♐	♐	26
	15	4♋54	18	23	8	14	14		5♑4	22	17	8	11	♑
	22	11 34	19	23	12	13	10		12 13	21	18	13	10	13

AN ARTICLE FROM POOR RICHARD'S ALMANAC

It included forecasts of the weather, household hints, information about astronomy, verse, and his witty proverbs, many of which later became famous. This publication became very popular and Franklin published it annually for 25 years.

SCIENTIST AND INVENTOR

By the 1740s, Benjamin Franklin had expanded his interests to include science.

A document he wrote on "promoting useful knowledge" became the beginning of the American Philosophical Society. It was the first society in the colonies devoted to scientific study. By the end of the decade, Franklin had become one of the wealthiest men in the state.

BENJAMIN FRANKLIN, 1778

BIFOCAL GLASSES

He decided to turn his printing and publishing business over to his partner so he could devote more time to science. He invented the Franklin stove, which could generate more heat than other stoves on the market. He invented bifocal glasses, which he used himself.

In 1752, he sent a kite with a key up during an electrical storm to prove that lightning was a form of electricity. Soon after he proved that his hypothesis was correct, he created the lightning rod, which prevents buildings from being damaged by lightning.

He made many other discoveries about electricity and he compiled them into a book that was published in 1751. He coined new terms to describe his findings, such as battery and con

KING GEORGE III,
KING OF ENGLAND

ELECTION TO THE GOVERNMENT

During the time that Franklin was pursuing his scientific interests, he was also working for the government. He joined the city council of Philadelphia in 1748 and soon thereafter became a justice of the peace. He became a representative of the assembly in Pennsylvania and in 1753, the king of England appointed him to be the postmaster general of the colonies.

In 1754, the French and Indian War began. Franklin urged the colonies to join together and he published a "cartoon" in his newspaper that showed a snake cut into pieces with the caption "join or die."

Franklin's plan to unify the colonies wasn't approved, but the colonies were getting uneasy under British rule and things would soon change in America. When the British imposed the Stamp Act on the colonists in 1765, Franklin testified before Parliament that these unpopular taxes should be repealed and the British stopped the Stamp Act in 1766.

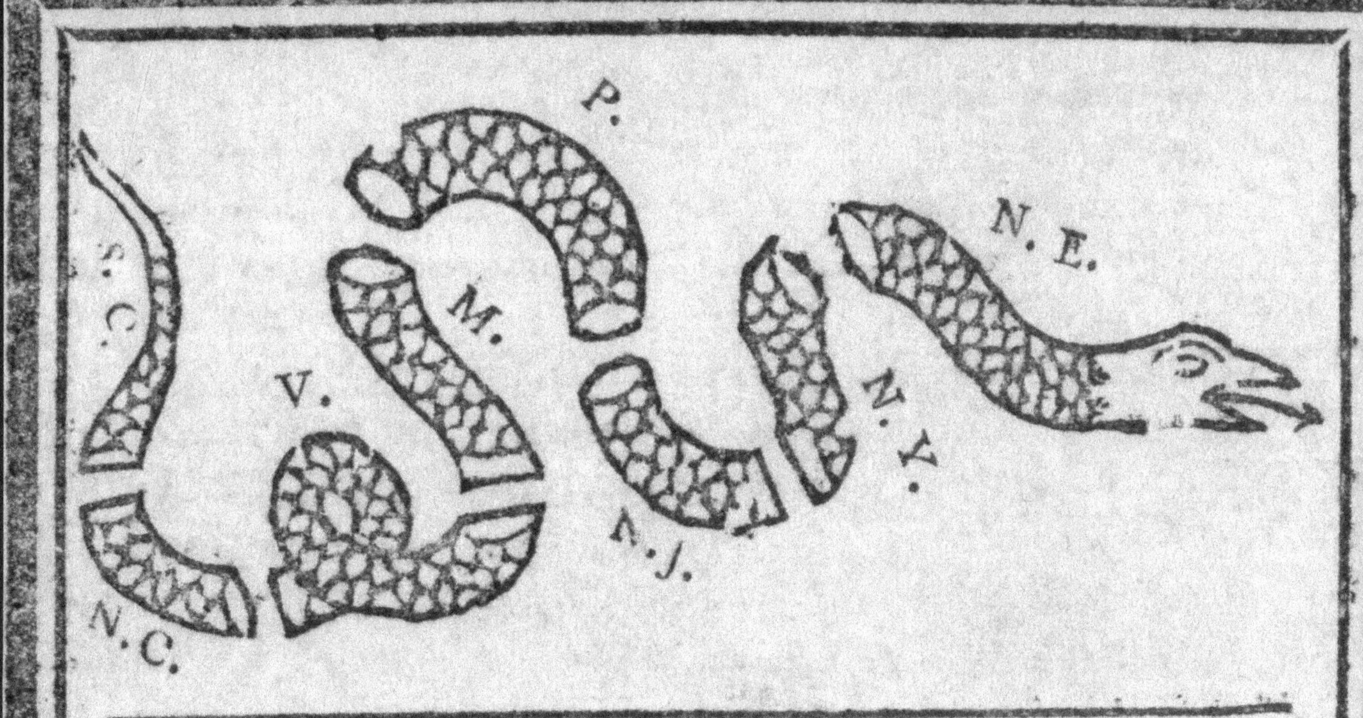

JOIN, or DIE.

THOMAS HUTCHINSON

Franklin furthered the cause of those who wanted the colonies to break away from England. He sent private letters from the Massachusetts Governor so they would be published in Boston. These letters from Thomas Hutchinson were about restricting the colonists' rights and they caused the patriots to get extremely upset. Because of the scandal, the king removed Franklin from his position as postmaster general.

By 1775, it was clear that Benjamin Franklin supported the cause of the American Revolutionary War. He represented Pennsylvania in the Second Continental Congress. He worked with Thomas Jefferson on the draft of the Declaration of Independence.

COMMITTEE OF FIVE, 1776

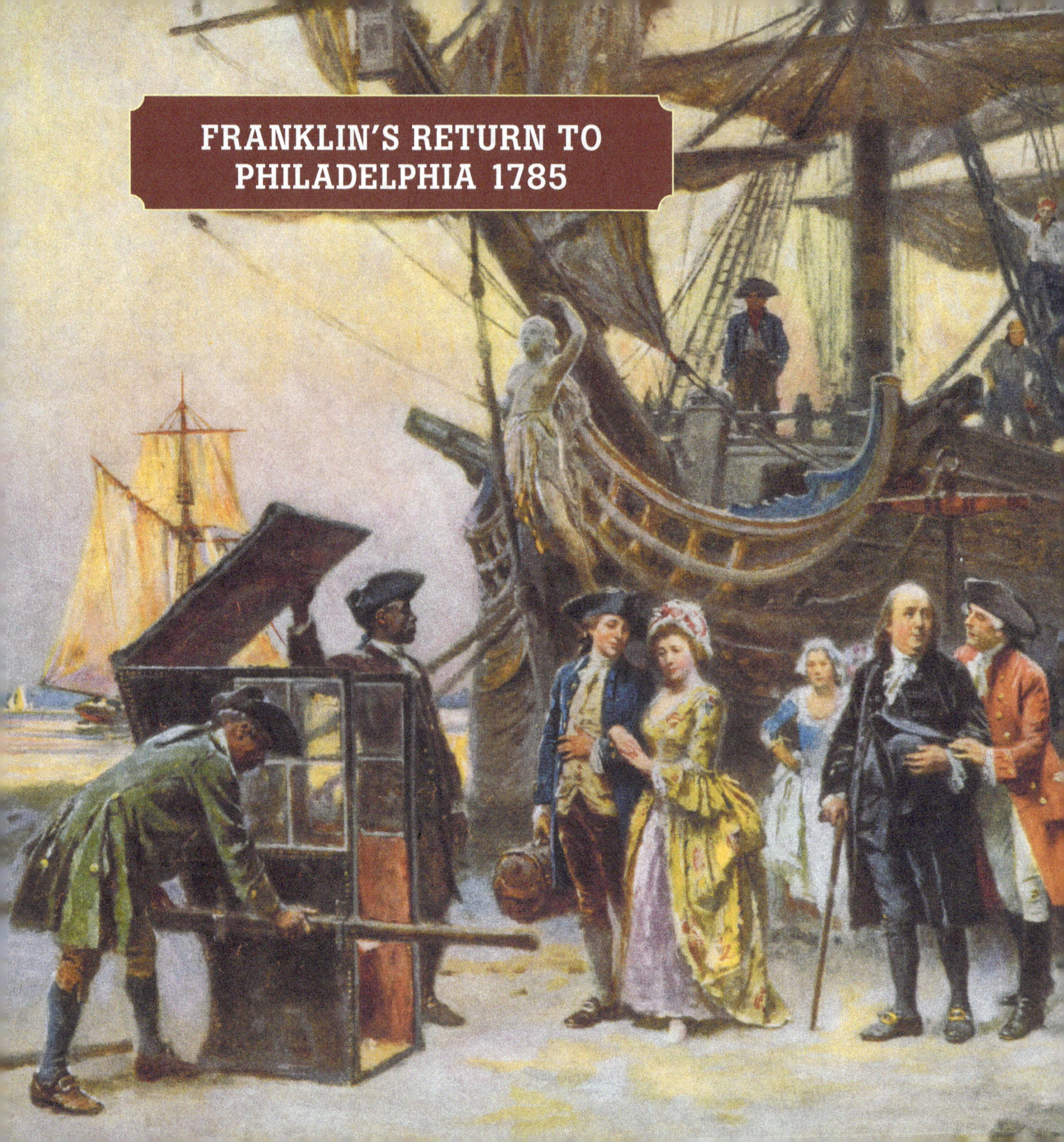
FRANKLIN'S RETURN TO
PHILADELPHIA 1785

Another important role that he played during this time period was he became Ambassador to France. He helped to secure the Treaty of Alliance with France, which ensured that the French sent soldiers to help the colonists fight against the British in the American Revolution.

WRITING THE DECLARATION OF INDEPENDENCE 1776

Benjamin Franklin became a Founding Father of the United States. He was the only one of the Founding Fathers to have signed all the major documents that were the basis for the new nation:

- The Declaration of Independence
- The Constitution
- The Treaty of Alliance with France
- The Treaty of Paris

When he died in April of 1790 at the age of 84, he gave most of his property to his daughter and very little to his son who was a loyalist and who had supported England in the American Revolution.

SUMMARY

Benjamin Franklin was one of the Founding Fathers of the United States of America. In addition to his roles as a statesman, politician, and diplomat who was involved with all the important documents of the new country, he was also an important scientist and inventor. As a writer and publisher he used his influence to further the patriots' cause.

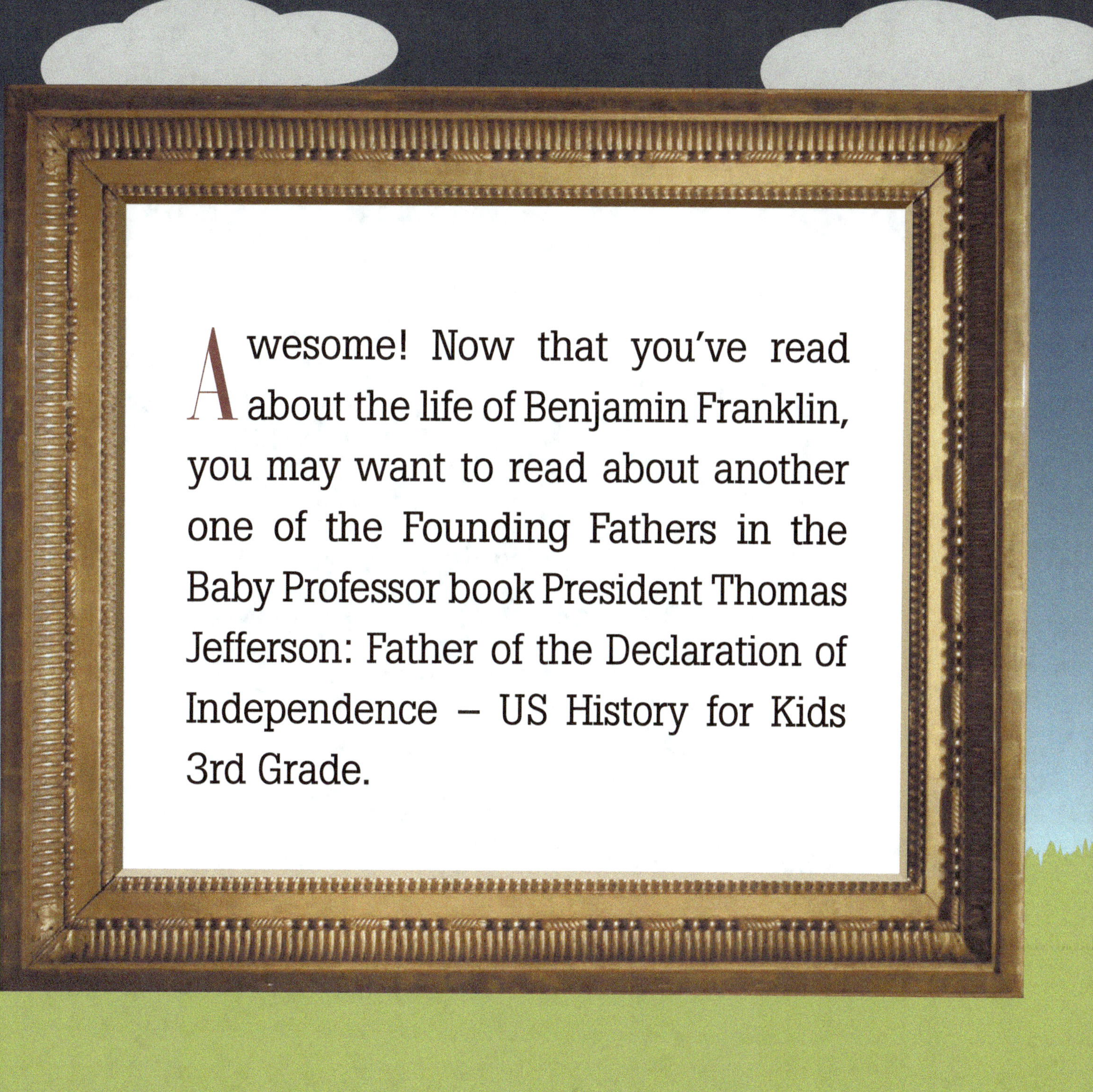

Awesome! Now that you've read about the life of Benjamin Franklin, you may want to read about another one of the Founding Fathers in the Baby Professor book President Thomas Jefferson: Father of the Declaration of Independence – US History for Kids 3rd Grade.

www.ingramcontent.com/pod-product-compliance
Lightning Source LLC
LaVergne TN
LVHW060508170826
845677LV00026B/1650